A FAVORITE CHILD PRESS

The Success in School Playbook: A 10-Day Program for Ensuring a Winning School Year

Laurie Boyd

@2016 by Laurie Boyd All rights reserved

All rights reserved. The owner of this book is granted permission to copy pages 2 through 18 and items in the Appendix for the purpose of instructing students with the *Success in School Playbook*. With this exception, no part of this book may be kept in an information storage or retrieval system, transmite, or reproduced in any form or by any means without the prior permission of the copyright holders.

ISBN 978-0-9969221-0-4

Kansas City, Kansas

laurieboyd@laurieboyd.com

www.laurieboyd.com

About the Author

Laurie Boyd is the principal of an urban middle school in Kansas City, Kansas.

Laurie has led many hours of professional development in the areas of literacy, classroom management, and instructional design and delivery. She also helped prepare hundreds of alternatively certified professionals to teach in high-needs classrooms in Kansas City between 2000 and 2010.

Laurie holds a Bachelor's of Science degree in Secondary Education Language Arts, and a Master's of Arts degree in Educational Policy and Leadership from the University of Kansas.

Other Books by Laurie Boyd

Beyond Classroom Management: Building Your School-Wide Discipline System

The Grammar Graduate's Parts of Speech

Table of Contents

How to Use this Material .... iv – viii

Success in School PLAYBOOK .... 9 – 27
(Student booklet)

The Success in School Playbook .... 29 – 51
(Teacher's Guide)

Appendix .... 53 – 63

- **Our Multi-Leveled School-Wide Discipline System**
- **Think Sheet**
- **Success in School: Test**
- **Answers to Puzzle on page 19**
- **Answers to Puzzle on page 20**
- **How to Handle a Power Struggle**
- **How to Implement the Program if Your School Has No System**

How to Use this Material

The Success in School Playbook is a ten-day school-wide campaign for generating higher engagement in, and more productive behavior from your entire student body, from the beginning of the school year.

As the adult leaders in our middle school, we agree that we want students to do the following:

- to attend school every day
- to follow procedures for order and safety
- to behave appropriately and treat one another well
- to manage their emotions
- to keep track of supplies and stay organized
- to engage in and put forth effort on their school work
- to be curious, to think, to ask questions
- to study and achieve
- to care about the outcomes of their actions

We know that we cannot take for granted that all of our students will exhibit these habits or behaviors. With this 10-day program, we address the common self-defeating habits or behaviors of our students, with firmness and kindness, from the first day of school.

Through this program, students learn the behavioral expectations for every location in the building: the classroom, the hallways, the cafeteria, and the assembly room. We also communicate expectations for our students' work ethic, character, and relationships.

This book includes several reproducible pages to use with students, as well as a plan for how to communicate all of these expectations, how to hold students accountable to these expectations, and an exercise for motivating students to know their value, to want to succeed, and to believe that they can.

If you are reading the electronic version of this book, you will not be able to copy pages, but I think readers are more likely to want to customize their own version of *The Playbook* anyway, using my pages for ideas, than they are to use the exact copies.

Even though you may not be able to use this material exactly as it is for your students, depending on your school's schedule and policies, you can take away ideas for developing a similar program for the first ten days of your school year.

If you have already missed the first ten days of school, you can reset the components of a positive school culture at any time. Use this material to initiate a special campaign to focus on the positive attitudes and behaviors you want to see in your students. Tie the program to a Thanksgiving theme mid-first-semester or to a New Year's theme as you return from winter break.

Getting Started:

We photo-copy and assemble a *Success in School Playbook* for every student. *The Playbook* within this manual begins on the next page and ends after the Stamp Calendar, with the words "The End."

Immediately following the end of the students' Playbook, *The Success in School Playbook* **Teacher's Guide** begins. The Teacher's Guide gives step-by-step instructions for daily lessons and activities, and describes how we implement this program in our building.

Finally, the Appendix provides additional resources and implementation tools mentioned in the book.

Preparing Your School's Customized Playbook:

Cover – You may use our cover or design your own. You may want your student booklet to carry out your year-long theme.

Large-Group Procedures – The first pages of the Playbook present students with a short list of behavioral expectations for every area where large groups of students interact – hallways, arrival, cafeteria, assembly venues. Decide what specific behaviors you want students to demonstrate during these times in the school day and simply list them.

While all of our teachers teach and monitor the procedures for the large-group areas, we do not have students memorize this portion of the Playbook during the ten-day campaign. When we see students violating these expectations, we call them to the side and ask, "Why did I call you over?" or "What do you think I'm worried about right now?" Almost always the student will respond with his or her knowledge of the appropriate behavior.

Occasionally, we will have a group of students who do not adjust their behavior to our expectations with these reminders. When that happens, we announce that teachers will be turning names of students who are not following our expectations into the assistant principal, and we guarantee the consequence for that infraction: "If you fail to follow the expectations you have been taught, you will receive a one-hour detention after school." It never takes us long to acquire near-perfect compliance. And for those few who never adjust their behavior? Well, they spend a lot of time with our detention monitor.

Incentives – Decide on your incentive system for the ten-day campaign as you work to establish all of your procedures and behavioral expectations throughout your building. We have found that our middle school students will do almost anything for Recreation – play time in the gym, on the field, or in the computer lab. We keep Recreation short (20 minutes) to keep them wanting more. Never let kids become satiated by a reward. It should end right when they are enjoying it most.

As you develop your incentive system, make sure that your reward can be administered daily and that you can transition to a weekly version of the reward after the first ten days.

Four Classroom Procedures – All of the teachers in our school implement a minimum of four basic procedures to ensure order and efficiency in their classrooms. We wrote each of these procedures as a title that begins with "How to. . .", followed by a list of five steps or behaviors.

Our four classroom procedures are: *How to Begin Class, How to Come to Attention, How to Borrow Materials,* and *How to Be Dismissed.* You can see the detailed list for each procedure on pages 29 and 30.

To create this page in the students' Playbook, just format four blank lists that students can write in beneath the title of each procedure. The

Teacher's Guide shows our completed Procedures page and includes an article on what it takes to embed procedures in your school or classrooms.

Classroom Behavior Expectations – Every teacher in our school teaches and enforces **five common rules**. There is nothing magical about the rules you choose. We wrote ours to cover any misbehavior our kids are likely to commit. You can see our list on page 34 of the Teacher's Guide, and you can read an article there about why and how we invoke these particular rules with our students.

Every teacher in our school teaches and implements the **4-step consequences**. We all try to enforce our consequences as consistently as we can so students can predict what will happen when they do not follow rules. Almost all of them learn to adjust their behavior so they don't get past a warning in their classrooms.

The first two consequences are fairly light – a warning or request, a moved seat, or a phone call home. The third step is a detention, given so that a longer conversation can take place between the student and teacher. The fourth step is an office referral.

You can see this list on page 35 of the Teacher's Guide, and you can read a helpful article there about how to implement each consequence.

To format the page called *Classroom Behavior Expectations* in your student booklet, simply give the title of your rules and your consequences and leave blanks for students to fill in the details as a guided assignment.

Recovery and Processing – This program requires a purposeful alternative to Recreation for students who do not demonstrate all of the expectations in your behavior system. Because they always go either to Recreation or Recovery, students are always choosing either a reward or a consequence with their behavior.

If you do not have a Recovery Room already, the teaching team should elect one teacher who will implement the Recovery Room intervention for all of the team's students while everyone else is in Recreation each day (or each week, later on). This teacher can use his or her classroom for the Recovery Room during this time. The other teachers can walk their students to this room for Recovery and pick up this teacher's students who are going to Recreation.

If you have a large number of students who need this intervention, simply dedicate more teachers to this room than to Recreation. Also, research shows that your strongest teachers should be those who work closest with your most chronic students. I have found that teachers who are effective with chronic behavior problems actually enjoy working with these struggling students and are typically very effective with them.

The administration or the teaching team must determine some more severe consequences for students who act up or fail to comply with the expectations of the Recovery Room. After all, this is the student's last opportunity to cooperate with the adults and the school-wide system, and to correct his or her behavior before an office referral and an office consequence. You must never allow defiance or disrespect in the Recovery Room.

You can read about our consequences for misbehavior in Recovery and our steps for processing on page 39 of the Teacher's Guide.

This section of the Teacher's Guide also provides guidance for using Think Sheets with students, for dealing with students who fail to take accountability, and for responding to students who lie about disciplinary incidents.

If you plan the responses provided in the paragraphs above, you may not have to change the formatting of this page in your students' booklet.

<u>Weekly Recreation or Recovery</u> – You will want to revise page 26 of the students' booklet for the specifics of your follow-through with the system. If you keep this part of the program going throughout the school year, you will be able to systematically hold kids responsible for productive school habits, and you will be able to ensure that more of your students stay caught up with the work in their classes.

Except for reformatting the appropriate dates on the stamping page (page 27), the rest of the student booklet can be formatted identically to ours.

Student's Name _____

Teacher's Name _____

SUCCESS IN SCHOOL
PLAYBOOK

SUCCESS IN SCHOOL

Large-Group Procedures

Arrival

1. Arrive at school between 7:30 and 7:45 a.m.
2. Line up at door when we open at 7:30 a.m.
3. Go through metal detectors and walk to your first-hour class.
4. While walking in the hall, follow all school rules.
5. No phones can be seen or heard.
6. No insults, name-calling, profanity, or bullying.
7. No physical contact.
8. Once you enter your classroom, you may not come back out without permission from your teacher.
9. You must be in your classroom by 7:50 a.m.

Breakfast

1. You must take 3 of the 4 items offered, and one must be a fruit or juice.
2. Once you take your selection, unwanted items may be left on a designated table for sharing.
3. Any items left on the share table are free for you to eat.
4. Teachers must complete their document for return with the meal tote.
5. Bag all trash from breakfast in the bag provided.

Cafeteria

1. Wait in line without touching anyone.
2. Use only appropriate language at all times.
3. Be polite to servers as you get your meal.
4. Sit at your assigned table.
5. Never touch anyone's food or tray.
6. Raise your hand and get permission before leaving your seat.
7. When your table is called, clear trays and trash.
8. Line up to meet your teacher for your return to class.

Hallway Behavior

1. Walk in a single file line.
2. Leave no more than one arm's length of space between yourself and the student in front of you.
3. No talking while passing in the hallway.
4. Keep all body parts and belongings to yourself.
5. No physical contact.

Assembly Rules

1. Demonstrate the acceptable hallway behaviors, as a class.
2. Sit where directed by your teacher.
3. Follow all requests by performers or speakers. Do not talk when performers or speakers are talking.
4. No boo-ing, jeering, or making fun of performers, speakers, adults, or peers.
5. When the signal is given at the end of the event, there is no talking – only a calm demonstration of hallway rules on the return to class.

Incentives

Recreation is held every day for the first two weeks of school. Your activity choices for Rec. are: basketball or dodgeball in the gym, selected computer games in the computer lab, arts and crafts in room 128.

Recreation Expectations
1. Rec. is not a right or a privilege. You *earn* recreation time by earning your stamps. (See below)
2. You must stay in the activity you choose for that day's Rec. time.
3. You must participate in the activity.
4. You must treat all adults and students respectfully.
5. You must follow all adult directions immediately and completely, including the directions to stop playing at the end of Rec.

Stamping – During the first two weeks of school (or of this ten-day campaign)...
1. You may earn one stamp for each of your classes.
2. To earn a stamp, you must meet all of the following criteria:
    a. No more than one redirect for any misbehavior (violation of any of the five common rules)
    b. Complete the assignment to the best of your ability.
    c. If you finish early, you must work on the extra assignment.
3. Immediately after each lunch shift, students will go either to Recreation or Recovery:
    a. All stamps? Go to RECreation, and have fun!
    b. Fewer than all stamps? Go to RECovery, and make things right so you can earn RECreation tomorrow.

On the first two days of this ten-day campaign, we will count stamps, but everyone will get to go to RECREATION. If you do not qualify, a teacher will share with you how to correct your behavior or work habits, but you will still get to experience Recreation for two days.

BEST REWARD: Acquiring successful school habits ensures that you pass to the next grade level with C's or better in all core classes!   WOOHOO!

SUCCESS IN SCHOOL: Study Guide

4 Classroom Procedures

How to Begin Class	How to Come to Attention
1._____ _____ 2. ._____ _____ 3. ._____ _____ 4. ._____ _____ 5. ._____ _____	1._____ _____ 2. ._____ _____ 3. ._____ _____ 4. ._____ _____ 5. ._____ _____
How to Borrow Materials	How to Be Dismissed
1._____ _____ 2. ._____ _____ 3. ._____ _____ 4. ._____ _____ 5. ._____	1._____ _____ 2. ._____ _____ 3. ._____ _____ 4. ._____ _____ 5. ._____

Classroom Behavior Expectations

5 Common Rules for Every Classroom:

1. _____
   _____

2. _____
   _____

3. _____
   _____

4. _____
   _____

5. _____
   _____

4-Step Consequences:

Step 1: _____

Step 2: _____

Step 3: _____

Step 4: _____

For the first two weeks of this program, steps 2, 3, and 4 will require you to lose Recreation and report to the Recovery room instead. Teachers in the Recovery Room will help you understand how to stay out of trouble and how to qualify for Recreation. They will also teach you how to process about behavior incidents with your teachers, as preparation for your success with our discipline system for the remainder of the school year.

If you violate any rules during Recovery, your consequence will be:

_____

_____

If you repeat violations of rules during Recovery, your consequence will be:

_____

_____

To successfully process with an adult about a behavior incident, you will be able to . . .

1. _____

_____

2. _____

_____

3. _____

_____

> The is the end of the **Success in School Study Guide**. You will need to fill in all of these answers from memory on your first required test of the school year. Your teacher will help you learn to study and memorize the information.
>
> To memorize information, you must **WRITE IT**, **RECITE IT**, and **QUIZ YOURSELF**. We have provided a second blank form of the Study Guide so you can practice reciting the information and quiz yourself.

SUCCESS IN SCHOOL: Memorization Practice

4 Classroom Procedures

How to Begin Class	How to Come to Attention
1._____ 2. ._____ 3. ._____ 4. ._____ 5. ._____	1._____ 2. ._____ 3. ._____ 4. ._____ 5. ._____
How to Borrow Materials	How to Be Dismissed
1._____ 2. ._____ 3. ._____ 4. ._____ 5. ._____	1._____ 2. ._____ 3. ._____ 4. ._____ 5. ._____

Classroom Behavior Expectations

5 Common Rules for Every Classroom:

1. _____

   _____

2. _____

   _____

3. _____

   _____

4. _____

   _____

5. _____

   _____

4-Step Consequences:

Step 1: _____

Step 2: _____

Step 3: _____

Step 4: _____

For the first two weeks of this program, steps 2, 3, and 4 will require you to lose Recreation and report to the Recovery room instead. Teachers in the Recovery Room will help you understand how to stay out of trouble and how to qualify for Recreation. They will also teach you how to process about behavior incidents with your teachers, as preparation for your success with our discipline system for the remainder of the school year.

If you violate any rules during Recovery, your consequence will be:

_____

_____

If you repeat violations of rules during Recovery, your consequence will be:

_____

_____

To successfully process with an adult about a behavior incident, you will be able to . . .

1. _____

_____

2. _____

_____

3. _____

_____

SUCCESS IN SCHOOL WORD SEARCH

Find the words in the list below the puzzle. They may appear horizontally, vertically, or diagonally. Circle or highlight each word as you find it. Check each word off the list as you find it.

```
S R H A T S U R T H N E D R A
N E A R R U Y S U O L I E S I
O C L R U Z D R I B S S S S R
I R L I T G T T A R P E T G E
T E W V H F N T U O M C B Z T
A A A A U E N P N B E N O A E
T T Y L T U T S L P R S F Q F
C I S E O I I Y S R U L E S A
E O D C V B R E C O V E R Y C
P N C E I P R O C E D U R E S
X A L L A R R E F E R E Z G G
E U I S E C N E U Q E S N O C
X T D W K I N D N E S S Q V L
Y G N I S S E C O R P Y P R W
V Q L E G N I N R A W N C Y H
```

ACCOUNTABLE	ARRIVAL	ASSEMBLY
CAFETERIA	CONSEQUENCES	DETENTION
DISRUPTIVE	EXPECTATIONS	HALLWAYS
HURTFUL	KINDNESS	PROCEDURES
PROCESSING	RECOVERY	RECREATION
REFERRAL	RESPECT	RULES
RESPONSIBILITY	TRUST	TRUTH
WARNING		

SOLVE THE PHRASE PUZZLE

The letters below each column are the ones you choose to write into the squares in that column. You want to form words beginning with the first white square so that you can read the message when you finish.

The first word is "RULES". Write "R" in the first white square and "U" in the second white square. Below each column, where the letter choices are listed, cross out the "R" and the "U". Continue forming words with the letters allowed for each column until you have solved the message.

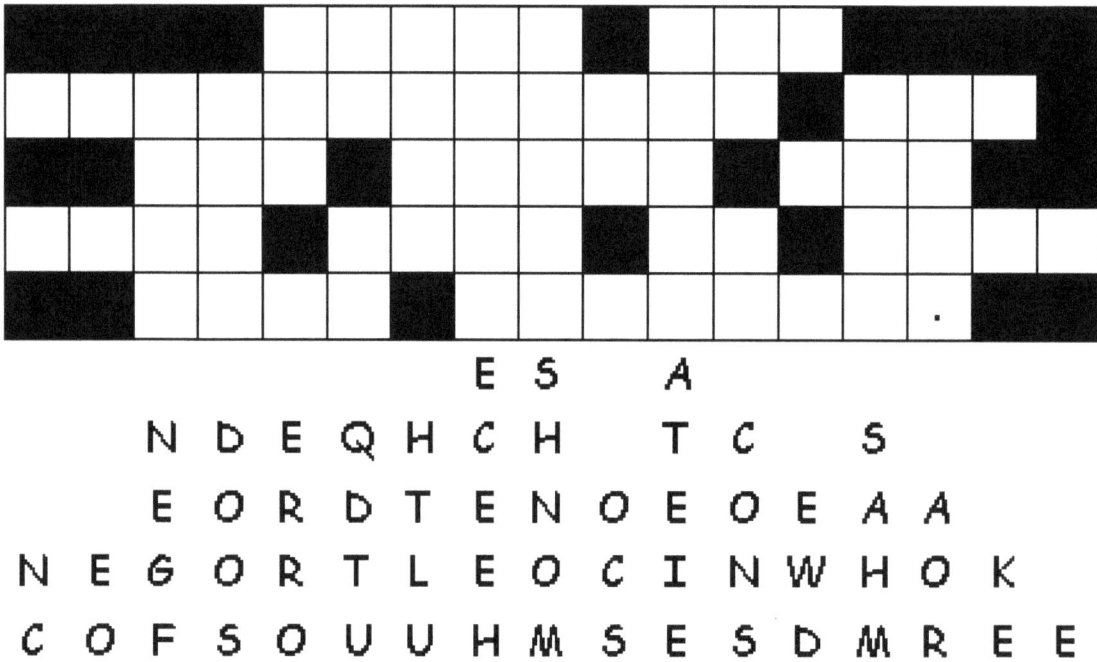

Clue: Rules and consequences are not for everybody. There are many people in school who already know how to act, how to show respect, how to be a friend to others, and how to manage their own behavior. The solution to this puzzle will tell you who rules and consequences are for.

20

Video Title: _____

Main Idea: _____

Details:

1. _____
   _____

2. _____
   _____

3. _____
   _____

Video Title: _____

Main Idea: _____

Details:

1. _____
   _____

2. _____
   _____

3. _____
   _____

Video Title: _____

Main Idea: _____

Details:

1. _____

_____

2. _____

_____

3. _____

_____

Video Title: _____

Main Idea: _____

Details:

1. _____

_____

2. _____

_____

3. _____

_____

Video Title: _____

Main Idea: _____

Details:

1. _____

   _____

2. _____

   _____

3. _____

   _____

Video Title: _____

Main Idea: _____

Details:

1. _____

   _____

2. _____

   _____

3. _____

   _____

Video Title: _____

Main Idea: _____

Details:

1. _____

   _____

2. _____

   _____

3. _____

   _____

Video Title: _____

Main Idea: _____

Details:

1. _____

   _____

2. _____

   _____

3. _____

   _____

Video Title: _____

Main Idea: _____

Details:

1. _____

   _____

2. _____

   _____

3. _____

   _____

Video Title: _____

Main Idea: _____

Details:

1. _____

   _____

2. _____

   _____

3. _____

   _____

CRITERIA FOR STAMPS
(During and after the campaign)

1. Be prepared for class, including having supplies with you and homework ready to turn in.

2. Do what your teacher says.

3. Complete your class work and/or assignments.

4. No discipline past a warning.

WEEKLY RECREATION OR RECOVERY

After the first ten days of school (or the ten-day campaign), we will transition from Daily Rec. to Weekly Rec. Teachers will stamp your Agenda, rather than a stamping chart, each class period.

On Wednesday, before Rec., your 5th-hour teacher will count stamps and assign Recreation to those who earned 80% of all stamps possible for the week. Those who did not earn 80% of all stamps possible for the week will stay in a classroom with one or more of your teachers for the Recovery process. Here, you will work on any missing work, or you will complete a Think Sheet and process with a teacher for any behavior incident that kept you from Recreation.

For two weeks, teachers will continue to stamp every class period for the posted criteria. After two weeks, for the rest of the school year, teachers will stamp more randomly, without announcing when they will stamp, so you must gain the habit of being prepared, behaving appropriately in class, and getting your work done in order to enjoy Recreation (*and* in order to be ready to pass to the next grade level at the end of the year).

Stamping Calendar for Beginning of School

Date	Hour 1	Hour 2	Hour 3	Hour 4	Hour 5	Hour 6	Hour 7	Hour 8
Aug. 10								
Aug. 11								
Aug. 12								
Aug. 13								
Aug. 14								
Aug. 17								
Aug. 18								
Aug. 19								
Aug. 20								
Aug. 21								

- THE END

THE SUCCESS IN SCHOOL PLAYBOOK:
Teacher's Guide

This playbook enables us to be proactive about our students' behavior and work ethic before they even have a chance to manifest the self-defeating habits of not working or misbehaving. Teachers plan a ten-day orientation to school that includes get-acquainted and team-building activities in every class, as well as the facilitation of *The Success in School Playbook*.

Our lunch block during fifth- and sixth-hour is our longest period during the school day, and no physical education classes are scheduled at that time, which makes it the best time to have Recreation in the gym. For these reasons, we decided to have fifth-hour teachers deliver the instruction in *The Playbook* and facilitate the incentive/restitution program in their fifth-hour classes.

Following is our implementation plan for *The Success in School* program.

Session One:

Teachers distribute the *Success in School Playbook* to each student and make sure everyone writes their name and their fifth-hour teacher's name in the spaces provided on the cover. They talk about the purpose and value of a playbook to a football team.

What is in a football team's playbook? What is it used for? (A football team's playbook defines the roles of positions on the team and presents specific running and blocking patterns for different plays to use during a game. It is the team's plan for beating their opponents, for winning.)

What do you think the coach expects players to do with their playbook? (They have to learn the plays and be able to do their part from memory when each play is called during a game.)

Why would we call our book about rules, procedures, and incentives a "playbook"? (It tells us how to be successful in the game of school. It is our school's plan for making sure we win at school this year so we can learn what we need to learn, and so we can pass to the next grade level.)

Let's see what's inside.

On page 2, we have five procedures for large-group supervision. One thing we have to remember about school is that no one is the center of the universe at our school. There are hundreds of students here. We have to have order to make sure everyone is safe and secure at all times. The adults will be monitoring you wherever you are in the building or at a school event. These lists tell you what we expect of you in these different locations.

Teachers read through each list with the class. Before each opportunity to demonstrate these procedures during the regular school day, they review the expectations again and monitor the students' performance of that procedure.

Teachers read through the Incentives program on page 9. When they read about stamping, teachers have students turn to page 24 to view the Stamping Calendar. If you make a similar stamping calendar, you will insert the dates of your own ten-day program, of course.

Immediate Practice of Large-Group Procedures

On this same day, teachers walk with their students in the hallway to a grade-level assembly before or after their lunch period. They review and monitor the hallway procedure, the assembly procedure, and the cafeteria procedure before students perform them. They give feedback to the whole group about what they did well and what they seemed to forget as soon as the class performs each procedure.

At our grade-level assemblies on the first day of school, my assistant principal and I welcome the students to our school. We overtly state our intention to make sure every student is successful with their academics and to make sure everyone feels safe.

I tell our students how much fun we have, how many privileges we plan, and how much support we have for them to master their school work. My assistant principal tells them exactly how to stay out of trouble, what counts as bullying, and what we are prepared to do in response to bullying and severe misbehavior.

I make a point of telling the students that all of the adults are on one accord with our behavior system, that it's my plan and it communicates my expectations (as building principal), so I am ready to back up their teachers whenever they need to implement the system. I also tell them that we are strict about their behavior because we expect them to be great people, not just good students, and we care about all of them.

Session Two:

The **Success in School Study Guide** is on pages 10, 11, and 12. Session Two covers our four common procedures for every classroom. Students write into the form every step of our four common procedures as the teacher writes them or uncovers them on the screen.

Here is the teacher's key to page 10:

Four Classroom Procedures

How to Begin Class	How to Come to Attention
1. Enter the room walking, talking quietly. 2. Go directly to your assigned seat, and sit down. 3. Prepare your materials according to each teacher's expectations. 4. Begin the assignment posted on the screen or on the board. 5. At the tardy bell, all talking stops.	*At the signal, give me five:* 1. Eyes on the speaker. 2. Ears listening for directions. 3. Mouth closed – no talking or noises. 4. Hands still. 5. Feet still. ("Freeze.")
How to Borrow Materials	How to Be Dismissed
1. Ask politely to borrow an item from a peer or the teacher. 2. Say "Thank you" when they give it to you.	1. Keep working until the teacher says it's time to stop. 2. Make sure all required work is turned in.

3. Take good care of the item that you borrow. 4. Return the item to the lender before the end of class. 5. Say "Thank you" again.	3. Organize your belongings for dismissal. 4. Pick up trash within reach of your desk and hold it to drop in the trash as you leave. 5. Wait until the teacher dismisses you. Then exit the classroom walking.

For details about each procedure and a description of how to rehearse these procedures until they become routines, be sure to read *What it Really Takes to Establish Productive Classroom Routines.*

What it Really Takes to Establish Productive Classroom Routines

Effectively communicating your expectations to your students takes more than announcing your procedures and listing steps. You have to get your students to practice the procedures, physically, in order for them to understand exactly what you mean for them to do. Otherwise, you are just another teacher talking about rules and procedures that your students think they already know.

Your students will wait and see if you really mean to enforce your plan. The depth of involvement you require from them to practice your procedures communicates how much you mean what you say. The requirements for embedding a procedure are:

1. Teach the procedure as if it is course content. Make students write the title and steps of each procedure, and of your rules and consequences, as you talk about how each procedure should look.

2. Facilitate planned practice sessions in which your students demonstrate each procedure.

3. Always catch students who do not follow your procedure and have them do over whatever they missed.

4. Once the majority of your students are compliant with the procedure, issue the consequences in your discipline plan to any resistant students.

Here is how I teach my procedure for **How to Begin Class**:

Students write the title and the steps of each procedure as I talk about how each procedure should look. Of course, the title and steps are projected on the classroom screen.

<u>How to Begin Class</u>

1. Enter the classroom walking, talking quietly.
   This means students will not bolt or run into the room. No one playing around or or trip their classmate. No one will push their peer. You may be talking. After all, I will want to greet you, and I will want you to return the greeting, but there will be no loud joking and yelling.

2. Walk directly to your assigned seat, and sit down.
   This means that I will not see Marcus, who sits near the door, back in the far corner with James before class starts, because "directly to your assigned seat" means that Marcus walks from the door to his chair, less than five feet away and sits down.

3. Prepare your materials according to each teacher's expectations.
   In this class, I want you to put everything under your desk except for the pencil and paper you will use for bellwork, your completed homework assignment, and your student planner. There will be no backpacks or books or belongings in the aisle. Please make sure everything not needed is stored completely under your chair.

4. Begin the assignment posted on the screen.
   When the bell rings, you should be ready to get to work on the posted assignment. Your paper should be ready with your name and date written on the top. You should not have to be told to get ready. Apply your thinking to what you are asked to do. You begin the class by getting busy. You don't wait for me to tell you. I have already started class by posting the bellwork assignment.

5. When the bell rings, all talking stops.
   I should not have to tell you to stop talking. I will know who has followed the procedure because they will have begun their bellwork, they are no longer talking, and they have out on their desk only the items that I have required.

How to Rehearse Procedures

To rehearse this procedure, I announce that we are going to play a game. One row of students at a time will go out into the hallway and pretend that they are just entering the classroom. They will demonstrate every feature or step of this procedure. The row that does it correctly will be the winner. I tell them to take 60 seconds to study the list and prepare to demonstrate the procedure.

Typically, the first row of students goes to the door and enters the room walking. They all go directly to their assigned seats and sit down. And then they wait, their faces beaming because they are sure they have done the procedure correctly.

I ask the class if they got all the steps. Almost always, the observers say that someone left their backpack in the aisle or someone talked or giggled. I point to the steps. "Are you allowed to talk as you enter the classroom?"

"Oh. Yes, you are."

"What did they miss?"

Eventually someone will point out that the students did not get started right away on the bellwork. Exactly. **And that is the whole reason to have this procedure in the first place**. I do not want to have to remind my students every day to come in and get busy on their bellwork. I want this to be a routine they follow without my nagging.

I ask every row to demonstrate the procedure. The whole class was very involved in evaluating their peers for the components of the procedure. By the end of this activity, no student could claim he did not understand the requirements for beginning class.

If a teacher wants to truly embed a procedure so that it becomes routine, her work on procedures is still not complete.

What it Takes to Establish a Routine

Even though I had clearly communicated my procedure, and every student eventually demonstrated the procedure correctly, would they all perform the procedure when they entered the classroom the next day? Absolutely not. By the next day's class, I was the only one thinking about the procedure.

If I allow any student to enter my classroom without performing the procedure, I send the message that I do not mean what I taught about my procedures. So I prepare to monitor the entry of the students, knowing I will ask many of them to return to the hallway to "try that again." Because I know it will take me all week to embed this routine, I am not discouraged or agitated that I will need to remind my students to follow the procedure.

For at least a week, my attention is on estabising productive routines more than it is on academic instruction. One of the most effective classroom managers I know explains that she spends 90% of her time on procedures and rules, and 10% on instruction during August, so that she can spend 90% of her time on instruction, and only 10% on discipline the rest of the year.

"Please go back and do it again" is the best way to correct a student who does not demonstrate the procedure. Over the first two weeks, more and more students remember to perform the procedure perfectly. As their peers get into the routine, the stragglers begin to adjust to what the majority of the class does.

What to Do with a Student Who Still Does Not Comply

Resistant students are those who purposely disregard the teacher's directions, either to get attention from their peers or to maintain control. Some resistant students just do not change their behavior unless they are made to change, through pressure.

When it is time for this intervention, I simply announce, "Nearly everyone is doing a great job every day with the procedures. Thank you. From now on, if you choose not to follow the procedures, I will assume you are choosing to receive a consequence. I will be issuing the step-based consequences I taught you."

As always, I have to stay vigilant to prove that I mean what I say. I have to watch for the first student who does not perform the procedure, and I have to . . . do what? Remind him again? Tell him to go back and do it again? Express my exasperation that my threat of a consequence did not get him to do it correctly? Threaten a consequence again?

No. I just need to follow through with what I said I would do. I tell the student privately, "Jacob, you did not follow our procedure today. I will be calling your parent this evening. You will want to think carefully about the procedures today. If you fail to follow them, you will be choosing to have a detention." Would this make Jacob follow all the procedures? I had to be prepared to issue the detention if he did not.

If Jacob struggles with letting an adult be in charge, he will probably argue that he didn't do anything wrong or try to assert that he did not know the procedure. Don't fall for the student's objections by trying to convince him that he did violate the procedure or by re-explaining the expectations. I would say to him, "Can you accept your consequence even if it's hard?"

If the student cannot accept the lighter consequence, I issue my next discipline step. "Jacob, you now have a step three. Your detention is today or tomorrow. I will make arrangements with you before the end of class, and we will call your parent.

If you have these conversations privately, Jacob is less likely to erupt. If you correct him within the hearing of his peers, however, he will most likely escalate, and you will have a power struggle on your hands. It is a hassle to have a power struggle, but you cannot be derailed by any student behavior. You have to be ready for a power struggle, and it should not affect you any more than a student who forgot to put his backpack under the desk. (You can read more about how to handle power struggles in the appendix of this book.)

How Long Does it Take to Establish a Routine?

It is easier, and takes less time, to establish a classroom routine if you start on the first day of school and don't let up until the routine is embedded. It takes much longer, and is more of a fight, if you allow students to do anything other than your procedure for any

> prolonged period of time. Why? Because your students simply do not take you seriously.
>
> The only way to change your students' perception of your leadership is to turn around and truly mean what you say. That means you will have to stop threatening and explaining and take action – swiftly and repeatedly – until your students forget that you ever let them get away with dismissing your requests or disrespecting you.

Session Three:

First, the teacher will review the purpose of the **Playbook** and then review the four classroom procedures by posting the title of each procedure and asking the class which steps under each title they can recall. You do this really quickly over the next several days so you do not have to ensure mastery right away. (You do, however, monitor for the students' performance of each expected procedure.)

This session covers the five common rules for every classroom and the four-step consequences implemented by every teacher. The student writes in each item as the teacher shares it verbally and visually (on the screen).

Here is the teacher's key to page 5:

Classroom Behavior Expectations

5 Common Rules for Every Classroom:

1. ____***Raise your hand and get permission before speaking.***____

2. ____***Stay in your assigned seat unless you have permission to move.***____

3. ___***Keep all belongings and body parts to yourself.***_____

4. ___***Keep your head up and eyes open at all times.***_____

5. ____***Follow all adult instructions immediately and completely.***____

4-Step Consequences:

Step 1: ___**Warning or request**_____

Step 2: ___**Phone call home**_____

Step 3: ___**Detention + Phone call home**_____

Step 4: ___**Office referral + Detention + Phone call home**_____

Be sure to read *What Rules Do We Need?* to understand why we use these specific five rules for every classroom.

What Rules Do We Really Need?

Even the most relational and least punitive models for school discipline admit the need for establishing limits for student behavior. The rules you publish, communicate, and enforce form the outline of those limits.

Some schools or teachers like to use the word "expectations" or "norms" instead of "rules." Since we all have to obey laws, follow procedures, or comply with policies in our adult lives, I do not shy away from the use of the word "rules" in working with children or teens.

Why Insist on Common Rules for Every Classroom

The personnel who work with students in alternative programs and sheltered placements can make better progress with our chronic students if they teach them to understand and respond to the same rules as those required in the regular classroom setting.

Common rules communicate to teachers my standard for classroom behavior. Teachers who struggle with discipline, then, have the same expectations for their students as those who find student discipine easier to enforce.

Common rules take the argument about rules away from the classroom level. Sometimes a student or parent wants to complain to a teacher that her rules are stupid or her expectations are unrealistic. The teacher can now tell the complainant, "These are the rules my principal insists we enforce. Would you like to talk to her?"

Here are our five common rules for every classroom, along with an explanation for why students and teachers need the behavior expressed in each rule:

1. Raise your hand and get permission before you speak.
When students are allowed a significant amount of off-task talking, their minds are on their social interaction, not on their school work. They cannot apply their efforts to the level of critical thinking we work so hard to get them to do if they are busy joking, flirting, clowning, and gossiping. Some teachers seem to think it is unacceptable for students to talk while they, the teacher, is delivering a lesson, but when it is time for independent work, they allow students to chat. Is the teacher's delivery to the whole class more important than their students' focused concentration on the learning during independent work time?

Sometimes teachers will argue that hand-raising gets in the way of a good discussion. They want their students to debate or discuss without the imposition of having to be called on. I clarify the use of the rule this way: "You are not leading a debate or discussion every minute of class. Sometimes students need to listen to you or to a peer during a lesson. Sometimes they need to read or write to interact with learning material. When you want them to engage in more authentic discussion, just tell them the parameters for the activity; that is the same as giving permission, so we don't need to revise this rule."

2. Stay in your assigned seat unless you have permission to move.
When I teach this rule, I show students how to enter the room and go directly, in as straight a route as possible, to their assigned seat. Therefore, I should never see students gathered in a corner of the classroom or any individual walking past a peer's desk that is not in line with that straight route to their assigned seat.

Because I expect my students to start class as soon as they enter the room, whether a bell has rung or not, they must sit down immediately and begin the work that is posted on the front board or projector screen. If I allowed middle school students to get out of their seats whenever they want to, or to choose where they are going to sit each day, there would be way too much distracting movement to accomplish much in the classroom. And that is the goal of each class time – to accomplish significant learning.

3. Keep all belongings and body parts to yourself.
This rule was originally written, "Keep your hands to yourself." Then I had to add "feet" when I found myself correcting students for sticking their feet into an aisle to trip a peer or for stepping on their classmate's heels as they walked to lunch. Shortly thereafter, I had to add "all belongings" when I had to address students' swiping at one another with paper or pencil, book bag, ruler, hat, jacket . . . you get the idea.

4. Keep your head up and eyes open at all times.
This rule originally read, "No sleeping." When a teacher asks a student to wake up because his head is on his desk and his eyes are closed, the student will say, "I'm not sleeping. I'm just resting my eyes. I'm listening." That's not good enough. We need for our students to be alert, to participate, and to engage with us and with their peers in order for meaningful learning to occur. So we require an alert posture.

5. Follow all adult instructions immediately and completely.
This is our catch-all rule, in case any of our young future lawyers want to haggle about certain behaviors that are not covered by one of our other rules. Adults have to be in charge in a school house. No student will be allowed to call the shots for long, if they try. All students have the right to feel safe and secure, as well as the right to pay attention to classroom activities and teachers' instructions so that they can learn. The only way to ensure all youngsters' security is for the grown-ups to stay large and in charge.

You will also want to read the rationale behind *Our Four-Step Classroom Consequences*.

Our Four-Step Classroom Consequences

As a teacher in a high-needs school without a school-wide discipline system, I wanted to figure out a series of consequences that started out with a mild reminder but could progress to an office referral. I was not one of those teachers who seem to have magic powers, who never need to use an office referral, yet their students are orderly and mostly quiet. But I definitely did not want to be one of those teachers who sends kids out for every incident. I needed some consequences that I was in charge of, at the classroom level, so my students would be accountable to me, not to my administrator.

Step One: The first time I had to talk to a student about a rule infraction, I simply gave a warning, a clear request to either start doing something or to stop doing something in order to comply with classroom expectations.

Step Two: The second time I had to talk to a student about a rule infraction in one class period, I assigned him or her to write 25 sentences. In our school now, we call a parent for step two. I do not expect teachers to drop everything and call a parent in the middle of class. They make a note of the student's behavior and call before the next day's class. A principal friend of mine decided to use a change in seating (inside the classroom) for the student's second infraction. All of these are suitable consequences for step two.

Step Three: The third time I had to talk to a student about a rule infraction in one class period, I issued a detention, for "today or tomorrow." Since we must call parents when we keep kids after school, this step combines the phone call with the detention.

Step Four: The fourth time I had to talk to a student about a rule infraction in one class period, I sent him to the office with his referral, on which I wrote, "Reached step 4 in one class period, for talking and playing."

Because my school did not have a school-wide discipline system, I went to the assistant principal in charge of student discipline and showed him my plan for classroom discipline. I described my first three actions and asked if a student's fourth infraction could result in an office referral. He agreed that that was reasonable.

> I asked what consequence he would assign for the fourth infraction. He thought the student should serve a day of in-school suspension. I asked if he would make sure that the student understood he still had to serve my detention for step three. I was hoping my repeat offenders would learn to stop misbehaving at an earlier step if they knew they would have to serve the detention even if they went to the office on referral. My administrator agreed to my plan.
>
> Many of my most incorrigible students did learn to stop disruptive behavior after a warning. Eventually, I could raise one eyebrow, and kids would calm down and get in order.

Session Four:

Session Four covers what happens when kids go to Recovery instead of Recreation during our daily Rec. time.

Students need to know "the bottom line" for every intervention. Recovery in our school is one of three behavior intervention programs housed together in one large classroom and supervised by three adults. The other two programs are Second Step / In-School Suspension and our on-site alternative school, School Within a School.

In Recovery, during the first ten days of school, the adults help students complete a Think Sheet about the cause and effect of their behavior. Besides small or large rule infractions and refusing to work, this program enables us to address the impact of losing or forgetting books, materials, or homework.

Several students lose their *Playbooks* right away and expect to be given another. We know that many students are careless about keeping track of their books and assignments, so this is a great opportunity to work on a new habit. Until they find their *Playbook*, they miss Recreation. (We will eventually issue a second *Playbook* or copied pages, but no more than one replacement, and certainly not before the student has had a chance to talk about this habit with an adult in Recovery and to look for the material they lost.)

Another habit we try to curtail early is refusing to working or not completing school work. Many students who have never worked in school start the year working along with their peers because of this program, and those who cannot maintain that work ethic get immediate help and attention.

Because we do almost all of the intervention through the Recovery Room during the first ten days of school, the adults who work with chronic kids get to know them from the first week of school. Our chronic students' earliest relationships are with trained adults who have significant expertise in behavior interventions. Chronic students realize that someone will care and help them when they cannot manage their emotions, their behavior, or their work.

The support from the Recovery Room is possible because our intervention programs are not full of students as we start the year, yet personnel for these programs are on duty. We had a full Recovery Room (10 to 15 students) during every grade level's Recreation time almost every day of our first ten days of school.

Because our intervention personnel were covering this piece of the 10-day program, the classroom teachers could build positive relationships with the majority of their students, celebrating good work and cooperation by having a bit of fun together everyday. Obviously, this allowed for the appropriate supervision of all students as well.

Here is the teacher's key to page 6:

If you violate any rules during Recovery, your consequence will be:

_____***Stay in Recovery until you complete a satisfactory processing about the behavior that keeps you in trouble in school.***_____

If you repeat violations of rules during Recovery, your consequence will be:

__***Office consequence, such as a required parent meeting, 1 day ISS, or 1 day suspension. As soon as you serve your office consequence, return to Recovery to meet the original expectations.***_____

To successfully process with an adult about a behavior incident, you will be able to . . .

1. _____***Speak calmly and respectfully with the adult.***_____

2. _____*Acknowledge what happened and take responsibility for your behavior*____

3. _____*Accept help with problem-solving how to be okay next time.*_____

You can read more about our programs for students with chronic misbehavior on my blog at www.laurieboyd.com.

Who Are Chronic Kids, and How Do They Impact a School?

Programs that Work with Chronic Kids, Part 1

Programs that Work with Chronic Kids, Part 2

Programs that Work with Chronic Kids, Part 3

Using a Think Sheet to Process a Behavior incident:

During the first ten days of school, teachers enforce the four-step consequences they have taught for violations of our five common rules. In addition to the consequences of the discipline system, any student who gets to a step 3 or step 4 for misbehavior in the period between today's Rec. time and tomorrow's Rec. time misses Recreation and reports to Recovery during Rec. time.

Whether a student is in Recovery for a behavior incident, for losing their Playbook, or for refusing to work, they complete a Think Sheet in Recovery. This is a form that requires the student to reflect on an incident, to take accountability for his or her actions, and to problem-solve about how to avoid trouble in the same way when facing simiar issues.

Recovery Room personnel look over the shoulders of the students as they write their Think Sheets to make sure the students understand the issue that brought them to Recovery.

Recovery Room personnel coach the group through each question on the Think Sheet. They communicate with the students as if they are teaching them something they don't know. They do not use sarcasm, and they do not exhibit frustration, disgust, or impatience.

These teachers realize that chronic students often struggle to take accountability for their own actions. They are not surprised or flustered when chronic kids attempt to avoid accountability. They are ready with questioning techniques to lead the student toward this skill.

THINK SHEET

Name _____   Date _____

1. What happened?

2. What problem did this cause for you and/or others?

3. How can you prevent this from recurring, or hwo can you respond differently if this happens again?

A reproducible page of Think Sheets is included in the appendix at the back of this book.

Students Who Refuse to Take Accountability

A chronic student typically uses a couple of strategies to avoid taking accountability. One tactic is to act like he really has no idea why he was sent to Recovery. He did nothing wrong; the teacher just hates him, picks on him, or was in a bad mood.

Another tactic is to blame everyone else for his behavior: "But other kids were doing the same thing. Other kids were worse. Someone else made me talk out (or trip, or push, or yell)."

If the student becomes stubborn and refuses to take accountability, the intervenion teacher will likely have him stay in Recovery for the remainder of the afternoon, even after the others have returned to their classrooms. The adult says, "I see you are not ready to talk about this. I'll give you some time to think about it."

Once each class period, for the remainder of the day, the intervention teacher checks back with the student to see if he is ready to talk about the incident. "I'll know you are ready when your Think Sheet makes sense, when you have written the truth and taken accountability."

This also gives the intervention teacher an opportunity to check with the disciplining teacher about the specific incident, and to ascertain whether the student has a reason not to understand the discipline or is just being oppositional. Either way, the Recovery Room teacher can help the student to problem-solve the issue.

If the student becomes angry and overtly disrespectful or disruptive in the Recovery Room, the intevention teacher simply invokes the consequences on page 6 of the Playbook.

If the student becomes cooperative, the intervention teacher finishes the conversation about the Think Sheet and prepares the student to "process" successfullly with his or her teacher about the initial incident.

We ask teachers to implement processing at a very surface level at the beginning of the year. We want to build trust with our most chronic students, so we want them to be successful with their part of processing from the first time they are required to do it. Teachers will simply ask them the three questions on the Think Sheet, and the student will simply read what he has written (which was pre-approved by the Recovery Room teacher).

If the student can do that much, whether they appear sorry or not, or whether we think they are fully changed or not, they are allowed to return to class.

As a student's issues continue, we become more intrusive with these conversations, a skill we learn from our BIST model.

When a Student Lies about an Incident on a Think Sheet

What if the Recovery Room teacher approves a Think Sheet on which the student lied about the incident in question. After the processing of the three questions, the teacher says, "You know, you did a good job writing up an incident, but this is not the reason you went to Recovery. I think we both know that. I'm going to have to send you to the office on referral because you did not tell the truth on your Think Sheet."

When she gets this office referral, the assistant administrator investigates the whole truth, re-assigns Recovery for the remainder of the day or the next day, and tells the student they must tell the truth and prepare to complete a successful processing with the teacher by the end of the next school day. She calls the student's parent to inform them of the incident and of her directions to the student.

She communicates this to the Recovery Room teacher and the disciplining teacher so that the disciplining teacher can go by the Recovery Room on her plan time the next day. If the student is not ready to process successfully with the teacher at that time, the student will stay another day in the Recovery Room. If he is not ready to process successfully with the teacher on the second day, the Recovery teacher will send him to the office on referral.

At this point, the student will be suspended for one day and return to Recovery to do what is expected of him. On the day of the student's return, the assistant administrator will hold the processing meeting in her office with the disciplining teacher, the Recovery Room teacher, and the student. If the parent wants to be a part of this meeting, we welcome them as well. The first ten days of school is a critical time to show, through actions such as these, that we mean what we say about our expectations, and we intend to work together in holding all kids accountable to the expectations.

So What Goes on in Recreation?

Recreation works best when students have planned, structured play time, not just free time. Because our goal is to build positive relationships, all adults (teachers, aids, para-educators) are expected to interact socially and have fun (play) with the kids during Recreation.

The grown-ups should be involved and interested, not just supervising. During summer school, our assistant administrators organized a three-on-three basketball tournament and a dodge-ball tournament for Recreation. Teachers played on teams as well. Kids love to have their teachers play games with them.

Our craft project consisted of cutting out words and pictures to decorate a personal journal. Once each cover collage was glued down, the teacher helped each student cover the whole outside of the theme book with clear contact paper. For days, the teachers worked alongside the students making their own journal covers.

These early interventions (positive outcomes for students who meet expectations, and consequences that include adult support for those who do not) require vigilant work throughout August and September. By mid-September, though, more than 85% of all students are demonstrating positive and productive school behaviors and work habits. Those who struggle stand out so that we know early in the year which students need our deeper interventions.

Session Five:

Over the next several days, for a few minutes every fifth hour, teachers show students how to "study." Most students believe that studying involves holding a paper with notes or some text on it, and reading it over once or twice.

We clarify to students that we can call words for hours, thinking we are reading, while we can be thinking about anything but the information on fhe page. In order to remember what's on the page, we have to "mess with the stuff" - to handle the material in different ways - in order to get it to stick.

Our tip for memorizing information is: ***Write it. Recite it. Quiz yourself.***
- We tell students they have to **write** the information (more than one time, and sometimes many times).
- They have to **recite** the information, to say it to themselves, to a friend, or to a family member (more than one time and over several days).
- And they have to **quiz themselves**, either orally with flashcards by themselves, or answering questions asked by a friend or family member, or by writing out a practice test for themselves and then completing it.

We include a second blank Study Guide in the *Playbook* for "Memorization Practice" on pages 8, 9, and 10 of the students' book.

Sessions Five, Six, and Seven

Teachers lead students through the process of *Write it, Recite it, Quiz Yourself* in a number of ways. One day, the teacher may have the students write the title of each procedure on one side of an index card and then try, together with a friend, to write as many of the five steps for each procedure as they can remember.

During this paired work, teachers can take the opportunity to teach expectations for working in pairs – how best to share work, how loudly to talk, how to stay on task. Here's an example:

How to Work in Pairs
- Write your own thoughts, ideas, or answer first.
- Take turns sharing ideas.
- Try to use equal "air time."
- Keep a six-inch voice / quiet conversation.
- Listen to one another.
- Think about what you learned.

Students could label another index card "Rules" and another "Four-Step Consequences" and try to recall those list. They have their completed Study Guide to refer to. Each student can use his or her six index cards to study alone or with a partner.

Because this is simple content, every teacher can focus on monitoring student behavior, compliance with procedures, and expectations for working in pairs or small groups. Unless we are careful to follow through consistently with our expectations, this work is useless. On the other hand, consistency yields really great results with the majority of the school population.

Sessions Eight and Nine

Students prepare for the upcoming test over the six lists on their index cards, which is the same material on the first two pages of their Study Guide.

On the eighth day, teachers may facilitate a game or contest over the content on these six cards.

On the ninth day, teachers give a practice test by asking students to complete as much of the Memorization Practice form as they can (pages 8 - 10). Students know they need to study whatever they missed, and they can correct their practice test using their completed Study Guide.

Even though we do not spend time memorizing the last page of the Study Guide, students may try to complete those pages for no credit. They are optional since the information applies only to the most chronic students.

Session Ten:

Teachers distribute a copy of the Study Guide as a test. (See *Appendix*.) Students must pass the test with 90% accuracy or higher. They all typically do pass this test with a high score, realizing that they can do well when they study. Teachers watch as students complete their tests so that they are ready to mark an "A" at the top of their papers as they finish.

Because they have spent so much time in conversation about this material, it is easy for teachers to reference all the procedures and rules during every class period, as needed. No student can claim he or she does not know what is expected.

Students gain a sense of security knowing the adults in the building are on top of every behavior and will manage each and every hurtful or disruptive incident. The majority of our students comply with these expectations and our year is off to a great start.

Pages 11 and 12 are puzzles related to the information in the Playbook which are included for anyone who finishes work early or who wants to complete them.

Motivational Speeches on Video

Our work with our most chronic students has shown us the importance of providing regular, intentional, relevant motivational speeches over long periods of time. We believe that soaking in positive life-coaching messages for a few minutes every day helps struggling kids change their thinking about their own emotions and actions and to consider better possibliities for their future.

We implemented our motivational speeches during our recent summer school for failing students, with great success, so we decided to try a version of this technique with all of our students during our *Success in School* program for the start of our school year.

Pages 13 – 17 are identical. Each page includes two note-taking forms for the motivational video series we show our students during the first ten days of school.

The teachers tell the class the title of the video and model how and where to write it. The students are to listen for three details or three memorable comments from the video. After they do that, they are able to summarize the title and details into one main idea. They write in the main idea in the blank. (The teacher can discuss the various details that students wrote down and then decide on a main idea together.)

Discussion is very basic. We simply ask three volunteers each to read one detail from their list. The teacher offers one of her details as well. If any student did not get three details down, they may fill in details they hear during this part of the session. That's it!

You can use this format for any short video you want to show. We really enjoy the motivational videos posted on youtube by Eric Thomas, known as E.T., the Hiphop Preacher.

Eric Thomas grew up in Detroit, Michigan, and encountered many of the temptations our urban students face. His communication style is direct and serious, but he is obviously a joyful, positive person. Many professional athletic teams hire E.T. to motivate their players because he is so real and so effective.

Kids and adults alike are inspired by E.T.'s messages. Here are the titles of the videos we use for our daily motivation. You can find them on youtube at https://www.youtube.com/user/etthehiphoppreacher, or on Eric Thomas's website: http://etinspires.com .

Day 1: What's Your Why? (3:10)

Day 2: Greatness is Upon You! (2:35)

Day 3: Secret to Success (Guru Story) (5:30)

Day 4: Surround Yourself with Greatness (3:04)

Day 5: My WHY Wakes Me Up! (3:04)

Day 6: Lion or Gazelle? (5:48)

Day 7: TGIM S7E6 Energy + Effort (10:09)

Day 8: Never Give Up (6:11)

Day 9: Be Yourself (3:35)

Day 10: Focus (4:38)

It is impossible to overestimate how critical these motivational speeches are to the process of changing a student's attitude, desire, or self-image. The teachers in my School Within a School alternative program make their students soak in these kinds of messages throughout the school year.

Before long, the students begin noticing and commenting on one another's self-destructive habits and negative thinking. They may not have mastered the positive thinking in their own lives, but they remind one another of E.T.'s advice almost daily. Over a short time, our most chronic students begin to demonstrate more belief in themselves. We watch hope and responsibility grow within them.

I incorporated the concept of the morning meeting around E.T. videos for our summer school, in which 85 students were set to fail their grade level if they did not do something different in summer school. Along with other components of The Success in School program, the motivational speeches proved to be an invaluable tool for persuading students to finally cooperate and finish their courses so that they could be promoted to the next grade level.

What Happens After the Tenth Day?

Page 18 describes the incentive program for the remainder of the school year. After the first ten days, we transition from daily Rec. to weekly Rec. The criteria for stamps extends to being prepared for class and doing what the teacher says, as well as completing class work and following the rules.

The final page of the *Success in School Playbook* is the Stamping Calendar, a chart that provides a box for every class period of every day for ten days. Anyone wanting to use this page will have to change the dates in the first column, of course.

We found that our *Success in School* program served to separate students who struggle with organization, emotions, behavior, or learning from those who can be okay and stay productive, as long as we provide structure and hold high expectations for everyone. The program gave the majority of our students a very successful start to the school year and energized the school family.

Instituting this program at the very start of the school year also quickly revealed the students who need the most immediate help. Our teacher teams began working on individual modification plans and behavior plans for these students, beginning their interventions before mid-September.

This early intervention results in a certain percentage of our strugglers becoming successful with their teachers' help and identifying our highest-need students. We have additional levels in our behavior intervention system, as shown in the illustration called "Our Multi-Leveled School-Wide Discipline System" on the first page of the Appendix.

Please visit my blog at www.laurieboyd.com to read more about our behavior interventions, our student motivation system, and our school-wide discipline system.

Appendix:

- Our Multi-Leveled School-Wide Discipline System
- Think Sheet
- Success in School – Test
- Answers to Puzzle on page 19
- Answers to Puzzle on page 20
- How to Handle a Power Struggle
- How to Implement the Program if Your School Has No System

Our Multi-Leveled School-Wide Discipline System

Large-Group Supervision

Arrival, Dismissal, Passing Periods, Cafeteria, Crisis Drills, Assemblies, Grounds

Classroom Supervision	Behavior Intervention Model for Chronically Misbehaving Students
Procedures and Routines: • How to Begin Class • How to Dismiss from Class • How to Come to Attention • How to Borrow Materials (Others of teacher's choice) 5 Common Rules: 1. Raise your hand and get permission before speaking. 2. Stay in assigned seat unless you have permission to move. 3. Keep your head up and eyes open at all times. 4. Keep all possessions and body parts to yourself. 5. Follow all adult instructions immediately and completely. 4-Step Consequences: 1. Warning 2. Phone call home 3. Detention + phone call home 4. Office referral + detention + phone call home	(Behavior Intervention Support Team – www.bist.org) Overarching Expectations: 1. It is never okay to be hurtful. 2. It is never okay to be disruptive. Like Skills for Behavior Management: 1. I can be okay even if I am angry (or overwhelmed). 2. I can be okay even if others are not okay. 3. I can be productive and follow directions even if I don't want to. Intervention includes: • Processing – a plan that identifies missing life skill(s) and defines target behaviors • Implementation tools - monitor sheet, practice, and triage • OCP (Out-of-Classroom-Placement) – student stays with trusted adult until he can acquire skills to earn back classes Non-working Student Plan: Steps teachers implement to determine the cause and solution for non-workers.

School Within a School (SWAS)

On-site alternative school for students who need long-term, intensive support to attend or remain in school and prepare to gain back classes.

THINK SHEET

Name _____   Date _____

1. What happened?

2. What problem did this cause for you and/or others?

3. How can you prevent this from recurring, or hwo can you respond differently if this happens again?

THINK SHEET

Name _____   Date _____

1. What happened?

2. What problem did this cause for you and/or others?

3. How can you prevent this from recurring, or hwo can you respond differently if this happens again?

SUCCESS IN SCHOOL: Test

4 Classroom Procedures

How to Begin Class	How to Come to Attention
1._____ _____	1._____ _____
2. ._____ _____	2. ._____ _____
3. ._____ _____	3. ._____ _____
4. ._____ _____	4. ._____ _____
5. ._____ _____	5. ._____ _____
How to Borrow Materials	How to Be Dismissed
1._____ _____	1._____ _____
2. ._____ _____	2. ._____ _____
3. ._____ _____	3. ._____ _____
4. ._____ _____	4. ._____ _____
5. ._____	5. ._____

Classroom Behavior Expectations

5 Common Rules for Every Classroom:

1. _____

_____

2. _____

_____

3. _____

_____

4. _____

_____

5. _____

_____

4-Step Consequences:

Step 1: _____

Step 2: _____

Step 3: _____

Step 4: _____

Answer Key for page 19:

Answer key to page 20:

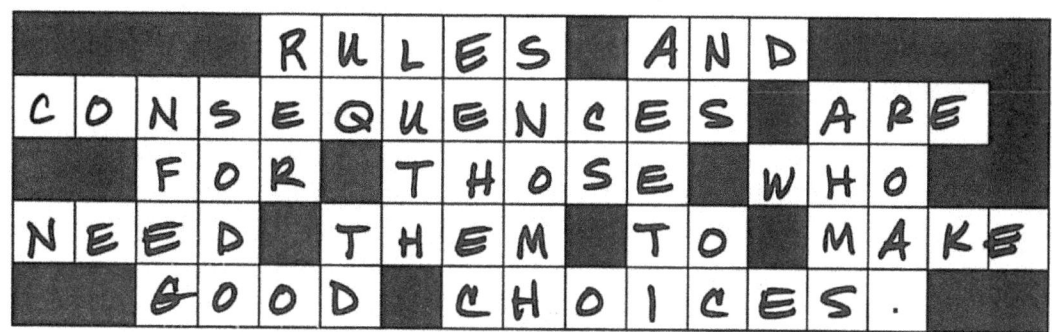

How to Handle a Power Struggle

How do you know you are in a power struggle with a student?
When you find yourself going back and forth with a student who is arguing or protesting against your decision to discipline, you are in a power struggle. When you are actually trying to answer, convince, or defend yourself against his or her tirade, you are in a power struggle. When you have asked or directed the student to pick up a pencil or lift his head off the desk, and he just won't do it, you are in a power struggle.

What triggers power struggles?
Kids who find it hard to accept criticism or correction often fight teachers to avoid the penalty for breaking a rule. Saving face in front of their peers, attention-seeking, work avoidance, and fear of consequences are all reasons kids object when they are corrected. Some have developed the habit of protesting or denying because it works for them at home. They can get what they want from parents by throwing a fit or pouting, so they expect that to work with other adults.

What do kids want from a power struggle, in the short run?
They want the adult to back off, or shrink away, or give up on holding them accountable. They want relief from being confronted. They want to appear "big and bad" in the eyes of their peers. They want to intimidate school staff from calling parents or following through on a consequence. They may want to get out of the room. They may be trying to set up the adult to look incompetent or unfair.

What do all kids want from adults, in the long run?
All kids want adults to hold them accountable without shaming them, to show them how to manage their emotions, to hold them to a standard that communicates we believe in them, to love them and stick with them even when they act ugly. Behavior speaks. Educators must learn how to interpret the language of student behavior.

What is the best way to handle a power struggle?
First of all, expect a power struggle now and then. If you have a student who struggles to let an adult be in charge, you can expect many power struggles. Don't avoid confrontations or shy away from them. In general, the best way to respond to a power struggle is to stop talking. Don't answer the student's attempt to bait you with allegations or threats.

If you say nothing, students run out of ranting energy in about 30 seconds. How will you make it through a hostile diatribe that may include profanity, anger, name-calling, lying, or threats? Pretend the student has Tourette's and look at his outburst as a manifestation of a disability he cannot help. When the ranting ends, simply repeat your expectation. Move slower. Talk quieter. This communicates that you are in control of your emotions.

Because we use a comprehensive behavior intervention model in our school, all the teacher has to say to an escalating student is, "I'll get you some help." The teacher then calls the office and says, "I need an escort in Room x." Our campus officer or any free adult arrives at the classroom door within moments to escort te student to the next seat in the school-wide behavior system.

Here are the steps to respond effectively to a student's escalating behavior, or when you find yourself in a power struggle with a combative student:

1. Move slowly.
2. Do not answer a question, a command, or an allegation.
3. Wait out the tirade, then speak calmly and quietly.
4. Repeat your redirection.
5. If the student esalates again, say, "I'll get you some help."
6. Call the office for an escort. Wait calmly. Do not try to continue teaching.
7. When the escort arrives, tell him or her where to take the student (to the buddy room, to Recovery, to the office).
8. Send a written account of the incident to that room, or send an office referral to the office, with a trusted student.
9. Resume teaching, in full control of your emotions.

Of course, we have a protocol at our school for helping a student earn the right to return to class. If you do not have such a protocol, your escort should take the student to an administrator, and your written document is an office referral.

How to Implement the Playbook
if Your School Has No System

The Success in School Playbook was developed for the use of an entire building, or even a grade-level team or an academy within a secondary school. If your school does not have a Recovery Room or an expectation of building structure as a team, you can only enact the classroom-level discipline and try to advocate for yourself, your fellow teachers, and your students by trying to convince your administration that your school needs structure in this area.

Meanwhile, you can implement many of the components of the Playbook in your classroom. In fact, you can establish procedures and routines, teach rules, enforce classroom consequences, and embed ten days of motivational videos with discussion. If your building does not have a Recovery Room, however, you will not be able to use that component of this program.

Here is what you might do instead: Use Fred Jones's Preferred Activty Time (P.A.T.) right in your own classroom for Recreation. (Fred Jones is the author of *Tools for Teaching*.) On two days, give all kids 20 minutes of your class time to experience a game or an activity that they all enjoy. It will be easier for you if this activity does not require your direct facilitation because you will need to spend some of this time in the near future with kids who did not earn the privilege. You will have to process with them around their Think Sheet.

Recreation can consist of 20 minutes of board games and/or card games in small groups in order to make it possible for you work with your more chronic students. You will want to teach and enforce specific procedures for participating in Rec. Here is an example:

> How to Participate in Recreation
> 1. Only designated students get and return games or cards.
> 2. Use inside voices at all times.
> 3. Follow the rules or directions of the game.
> 4. No arguing. If you cannot solve your issue quietly and fairly, you will lose Rec. for the day.
> 5. Any student may opt to read a book instead of playing a game during Rec.
> 6. You / Your group must stick with your choice throughout this day's Rec.

After the two sessions of free Rec., students must earn their stamps to participate in Recreation. First, move students who elect to read instead of play a game to an area designated for readers. Second, move students who must complete a Think Sheet and process with you to a table or set of desks that you will join once everyone else is involved in their game.

Have the game-playing students arrange their desks into groups of four, or fewer. Each group randomly draws a number to determine the order in which they will choose a game. The materials person picks up the game and orchestrates the set-up and the start of play.

For the first few minutes of the play time, monitor all students for compliance with the procedure for How to Participate in Recreation. If you have to correct an individual or a group more than twice, make them put their game away and read or rest silently for the remainder of the time.

Sit with your students who did not earn Rec. and kindly but firmly require them to fill out the Think Sheet. You will almost always need to teach and reinforce the appropriate completion of a Think Sheet. Once the Think Sheet is completed, go through it with the student by simply verbalizing the printed Think Sheet questions and having him or her verbalize their written answers.

As soon as processing is complete, ask each student if they want to read silently or just rest for the remainder of Rec. Remind them that from this time forward, they are working on earning tomorrow's (or next week's) Recreation.

If a student becomes oppositional or uncooperative during this time, begin to issue the four-step consequences for their infraction of rule #5: *Follow all adult instructions immediately and completely*.

If you have few or no students with which to process, you may want to facilitate a more active whole-class game or competition. If you have an opportunity to use the gym or go outside, you might take advantage of that opportunity, as long as you have been fully successful in embedding the routine for appropriate participation in Recreation.

Please be mindful of the following traps. If you, as the adult in charge, commit any of these blunders, you will undermine and destroy all of the positive outcomes you hoped to accomplish with this program:

1. Never give Rec. to anyone who did not earn it.
2. Never allow anyone to participate in Rec. inappropriately. Even If you have to have everyone resting throughout the remainder of the designated time period, don't allow Rec. to continue with any inappropriate behavior.
3. Do not allow kids who did not earn Rec. to skip the Think Sheet or processing.
4. Follow through to issue consequences if anyone misbehaves during Rec. or processing.

Laurie Boyd creates resources for educators
in the areas of . . .

- Classroom Management
- School-Wide Discipline Systems
- School-Wide Motivational Systems
- Writing Instruction
- School Leadership

Grab your FREE *Comprehensive Classroom Management Guide* **at www.laurieboyd.com**

www.ingramcontent.com/pod-product-compliance
Lightning Source LLC
Chambersburg PA
CBHW081455060426

42444CB00037BA/3301